DEDICATION

To my coworkers, who laughed along (or at least pretended to) through years of my Friday joke emails. This book is as much your fault as mine.

To my amazing wife, for her unwavering support, and to my daughter, who always reminds me how important laughter really is.

And finally to my late grandfather, a true jokester at heart - this one's in your honor.

Have a delightfully terrible electrical joke?

Email it to matt@engineer-injokes.com

or visit www.engineer-injokes.com

If it's as shockingly cringe-worthy as the ones in here,
it could just make it into the next volume!

WHY DID THE ELECTRICAL ENGINEER CROSS THE ROAD?

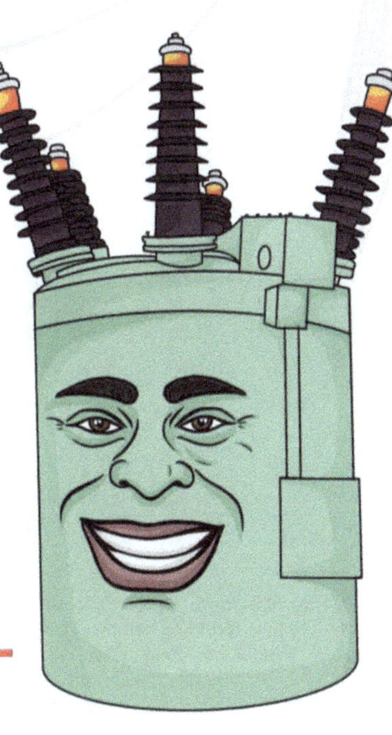

ISBN: 9798346944164

This book is a work of humor and intended for entertainment purposes only.

CONTENTS

CHAPTER 1

What do you call a current transformer in heavy rain?

Saturated.

What do you call a fuse that left school before graduating?

A drop-out.

Why was the circuit breaker on the run from the police?

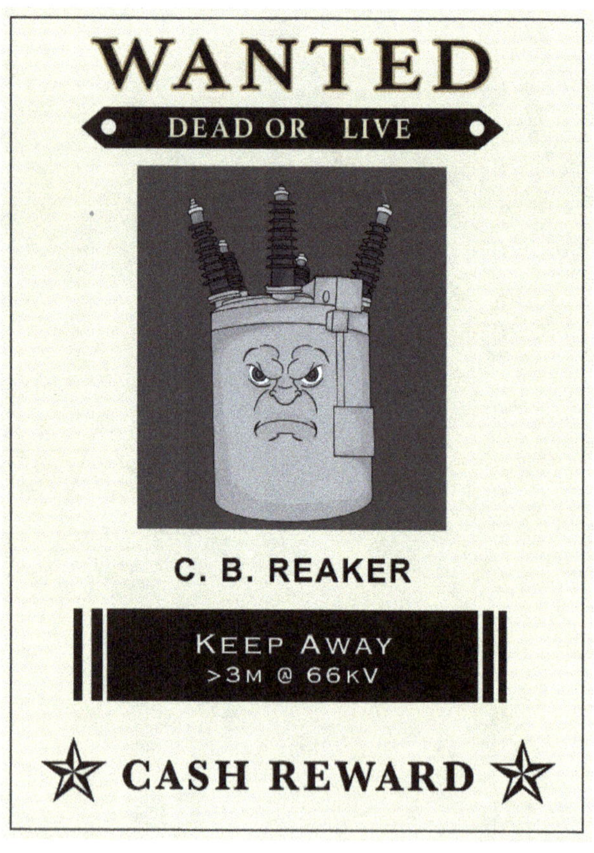

It was wanted: dead or live.

Why do motors need cooling systems?

Many fans make light work.

Why did the distance relay grow a moustache?

It was Mho-vember.

How would you describe the personality of a ground conductor?

Down to earth.

Why do differential relays always travel with distance relays?

For backup protection.

How does a circuit breaker prepare its meals?

Make before bake.

How was the cable laid to rest at their funeral?

Dead and direct buried.

What do you call a circuit breaker wearing a crown?

The Amperor.

What was the crown made of?

Joules.

What did the underfrequency relay say when it was dropped?

That Hertz.

Why did the auxiliary relay go to the optometrist?

Because it lost its contacts.

Why did the binary input lose its job?

It was always high.

Why was the overvoltage relay promoted?

It had lots of potential.

Why was the undervoltage relay demoted?

It had a loss of potential.

What gender did the electromechanical relay identify as?

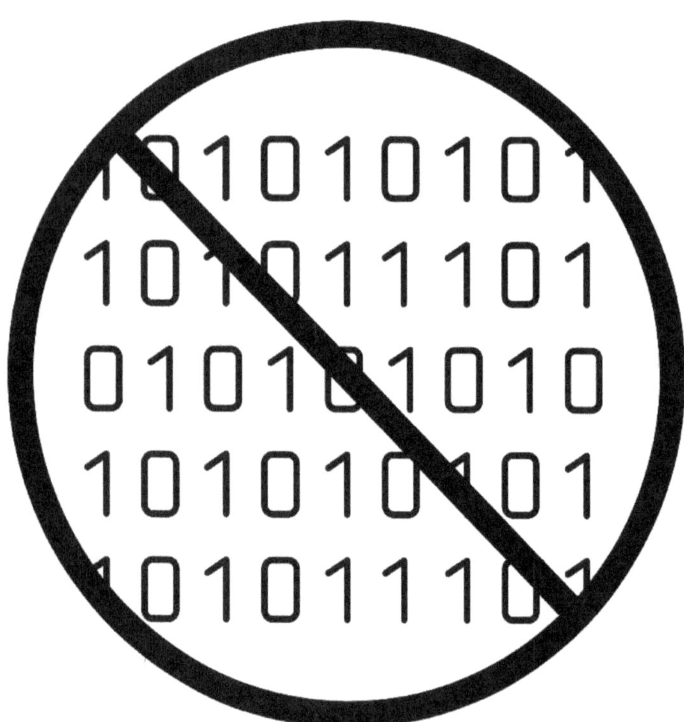

Non-binary.

What do you call an inactive protection relay?

A CBF relay.

Why did the electron go up the mountain?

To Coloumb to the top.

What instrument does a cable play?

The drums.

Why did the battery jump?

It got a boost.

Why did the transformer call the plumber?

It needed a tap changer.

Why did the generator call the plumber?

It needed a synch check.

Why was the transformer so happy?

Over-excitation.

What is a digital relay's favorite snack?

Micro-chips.

How do generators communicate?

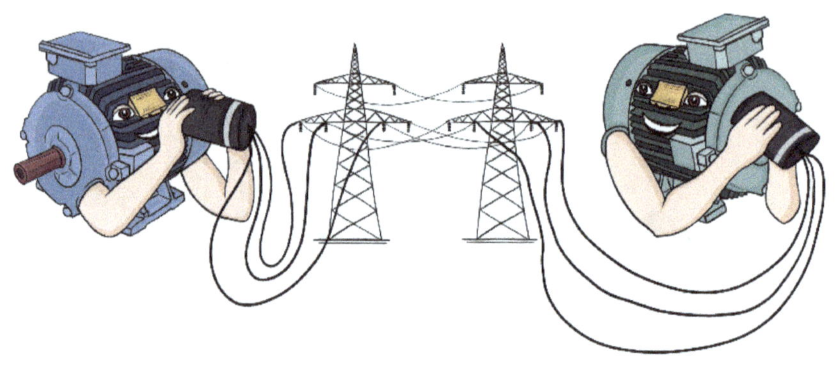

They torque.

Why did one transformer mimic the other?

It was a matching transformer.

Why was the overcurrent relay always late?

It was time-delayed.

Why was the DC transformer not allowed on site?

It didn't have the proper induction.

Why was the circuit breaker's restaurant always empty?

It was normally closed.

Why are push buttons so easily aroused?

They turn on with momentary contact.

Why did the upstream relay always blame the downstream relay?

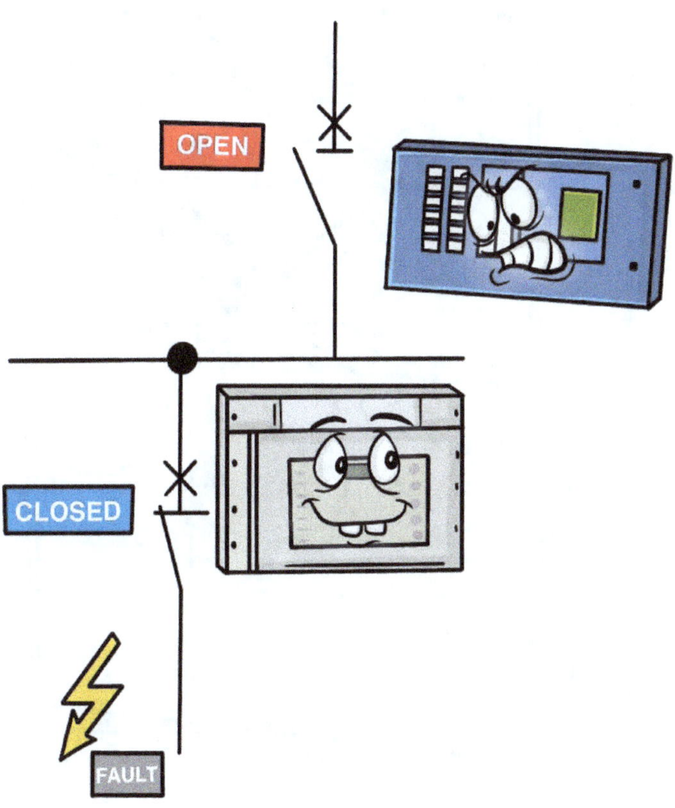

Because it wasn't their fault.

Why was the RMU angry?

It had a short fuse.

Why was the fault current running a marathon?

It was a cross-country fault.

Why did the battery go to prison?

Battery.

How was the battery released from prison?

It was discharged.

Why was the electron so happy?

It was having a field day.

How do electrons get to school?

The bus.

Why was the capacitor bank protection relay washed out to sea?

Undercurrent.

Why did the circuit breaker feel sad?

It was isolated.

Why do harmonic filter banks hate loud music?

Too much noise.

What do you call a shy motor?

A soft-starter.

What do you call a conductor sitting on the fence?

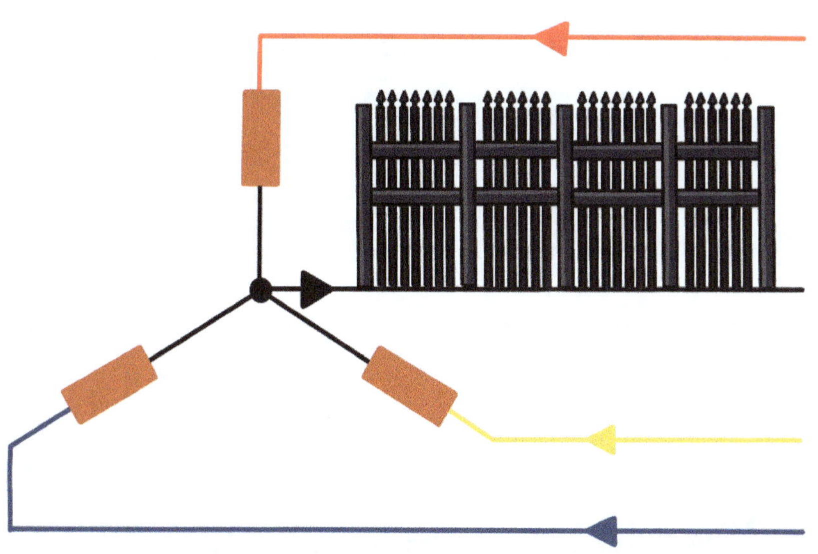

A neutral conductor.

Why do RTU's always work overtime?

Because they work around the clock.

—/\/\/— ⏚ —||||— —▷|— —ooo— —/\/\/— ⏚ —||||— —▷|— —ooo— —/\/\/— ⏚ —||||—

Why did the ethernet switch go to the work conference?

To network.

What do you call a transformer who quits their job?

A step-down transformer.

What cable type would you find in a mental asylum?

A twisted-pair.

Why was the transformer frustrated?

It was wound the wrong way.

Why did the motor fall over?

Loss of balance.

Why are quality loads hard to find?

They're few and VAR between.

Why did the circuit breaker need a holiday?

It was always overloaded.

Why did the distance relay quit smoking?

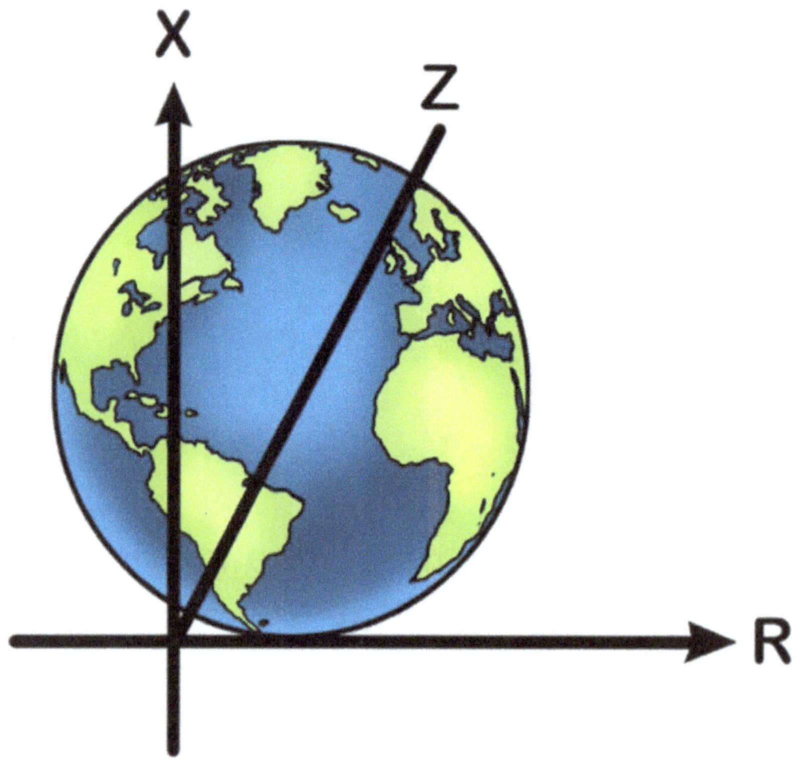

To protect the mho-zone.

How would you describe 100 MVAr of load?

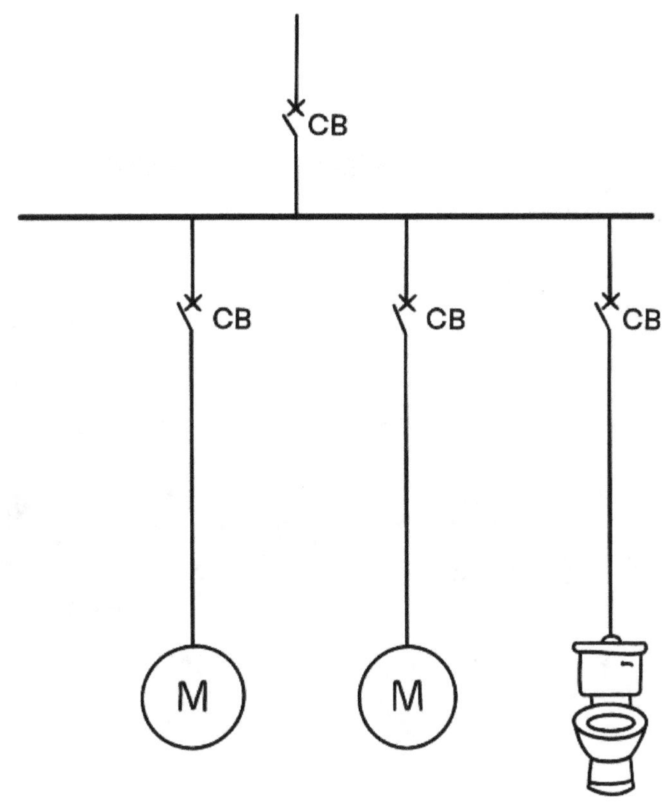

A shit load.

Why did the generator need an outage?

To take a load off.

Why was the overcurrent relay with the wrong crowd?

It was non-directional.

What do you call an emotional earth fault?

A sensitive earth fault.

Why did the network switch cross the road?

To stop traffic.

What pet did the digital relay own?

A watch-dog.

What happened to the transformer who misbehaved?

It was grounded.

What footwear did the digital relay wear to the beach?

Flip-flops.

How can you tell when an auxiliary relay is aroused?

Its contacts are wet.

CHAPTER 2

Why did the overcurrent relay go to the night club?

To pickup.

What do you call conductors in a relationship?

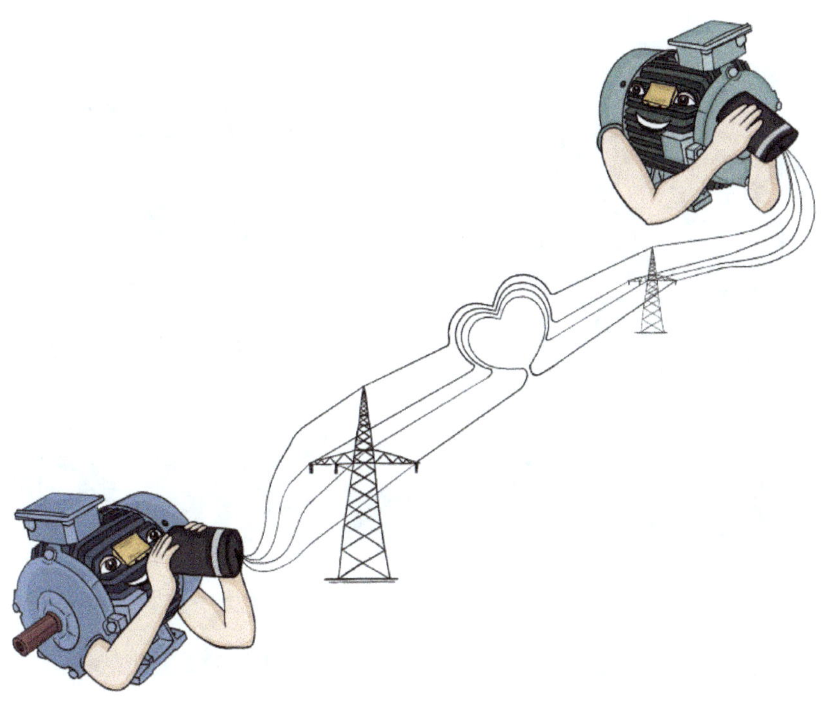

Mutually coupled.

Why did the differential relays get a divorce?

Comms failure.

Why were the two parallelled Dyn transformers unified?

Because they shared a common ground.

Why do distance relays struggle to stay married?

Long-distance relationships rarely work out.

Why do capacitor bank's often break up?

They are over-reactive.

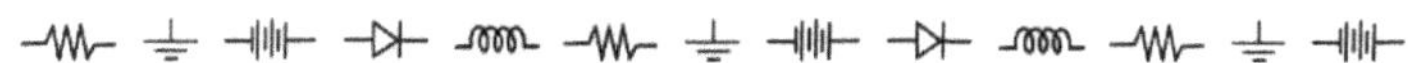

What caused the network switches to break up?

Mixed signals and cross-talk.

Why did the protection relay apologize?

Because it was their fault.

Why were the batteries so fond of each other?

They were BESS friends.

What does a digital relay use for contraception?

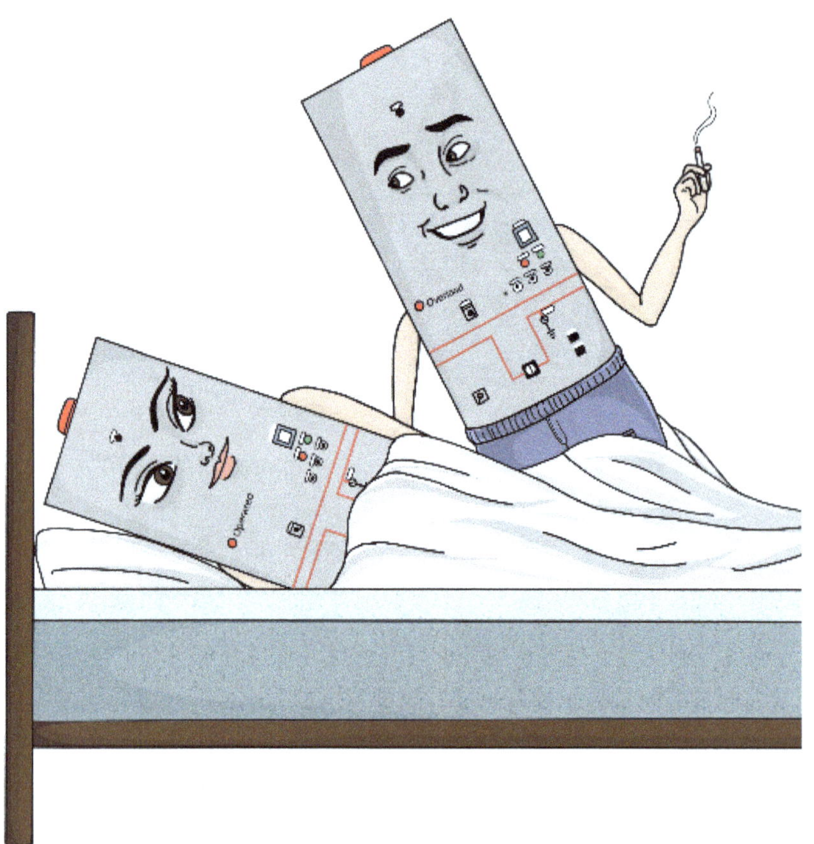

Leakage protection.

Why did the digital relay have an erection problem?

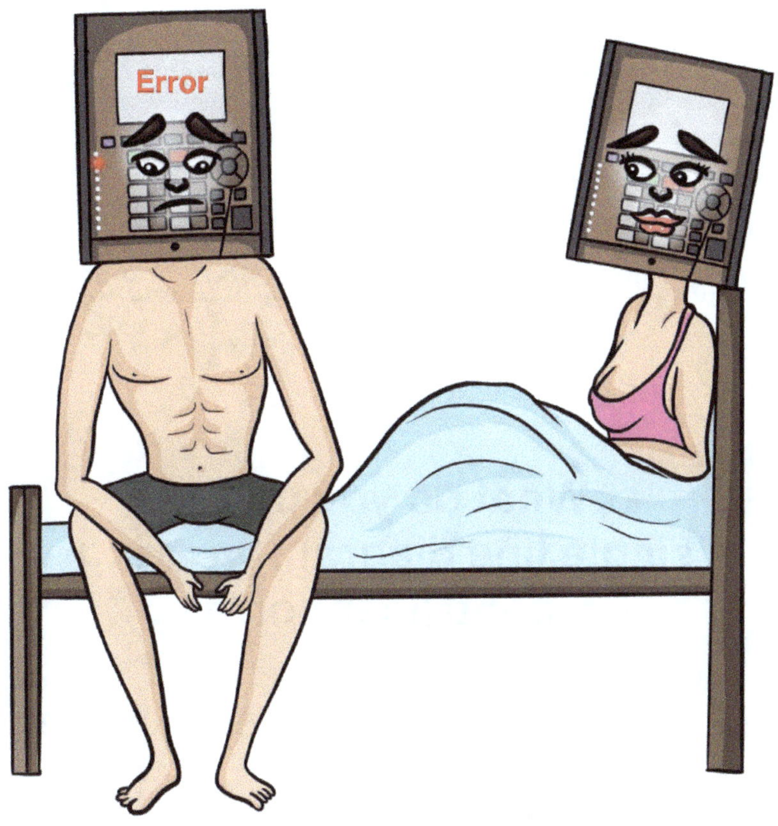

Hardware fail.

What do you call a single line diagram with a wife?

A married line diagram.

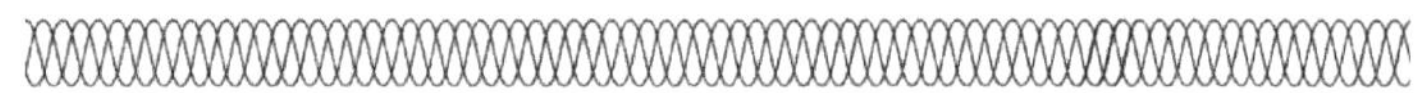

What do you call a single line diagram wearing contraception?

A protection single line diagram.

What do you call a transformer's marriage counselor?

A regulator.

Why did the tap changers get a divorce?

One kept running away.

What did one generator say to the other?

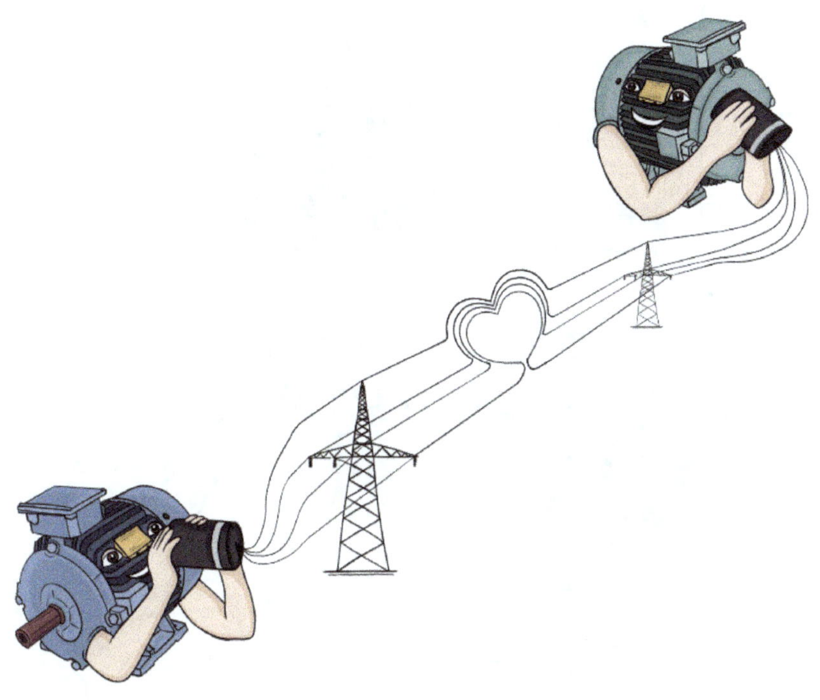

I can't stop synching of you.

How did the protection panel propose?

It got a ring out.

CHAPTER 3

What is an Arc Suppression Coil's favorite movie?

Silence of the Amps.

What is a resistor's favorite movie?

Ohm Alone.

Why do generators enjoy Game of Thrones?

Because of the power swings.

What is a motor's least favorite movie?

Pulp Friction.

What is a transformer's favorite movie?

.... Transformers.

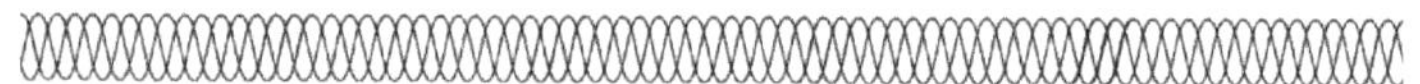

What is a transformer’s second favorite movie?

Gone with the Winding.

What is an insulator's favorite movie?

Ion Man.

What is an insulator's second favorite movie?

The Ion King.

What is an insulator's third favorite movie?

Saving Private Ion.

What is a transformer's favorite television show?

Dancing with the Delta-stars.

What is a SCADA engineer's favorite movie?

Switchy Switch.

What is a rectifier's favorite band?

AC/DC.

What is an ammeter's favorite show?

A current affair.

What is a motor's least favorite movie?

Phase-Off.

Which actor starred in that movie?

Nicholas Squirrel-Cage.

Which other actor starred in that movie?

John Tra-volt-a.

What is a switchboard's favorite movie?

Raiders of the Lost Arc Fault.

What is a generator's favorite movie?

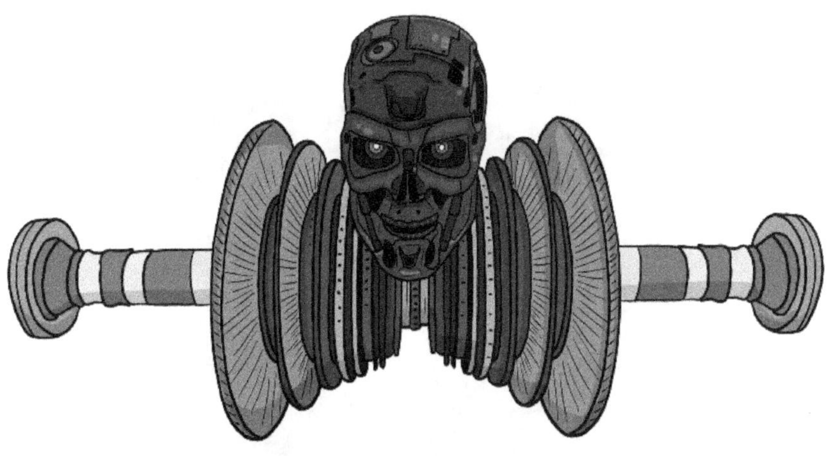

The Turbine-ator.

Who is a switchboard's favorite actor?

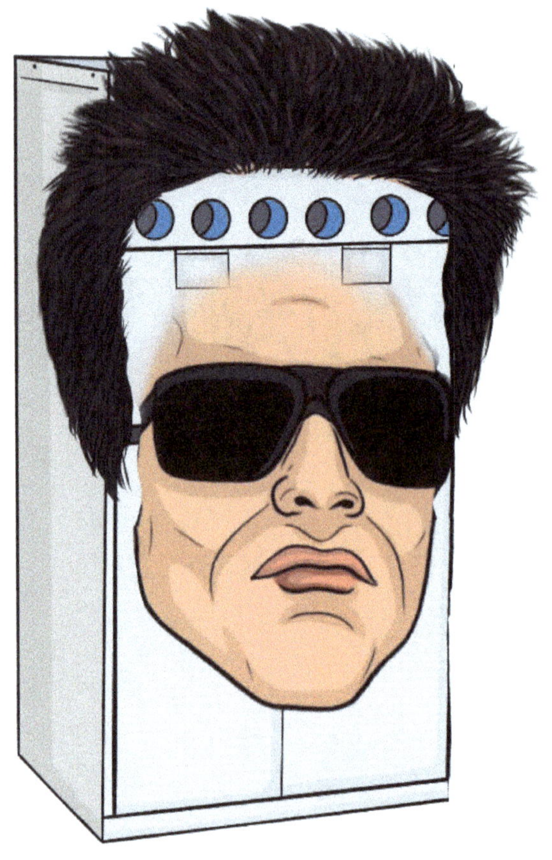

Arnold Schwarze-megger.

What is a transmission line's favorite television show?

The X/R Factor.

What is a reactor's favorite movie?

Good Will Shunting.

What is a protection panel's favorite television show?

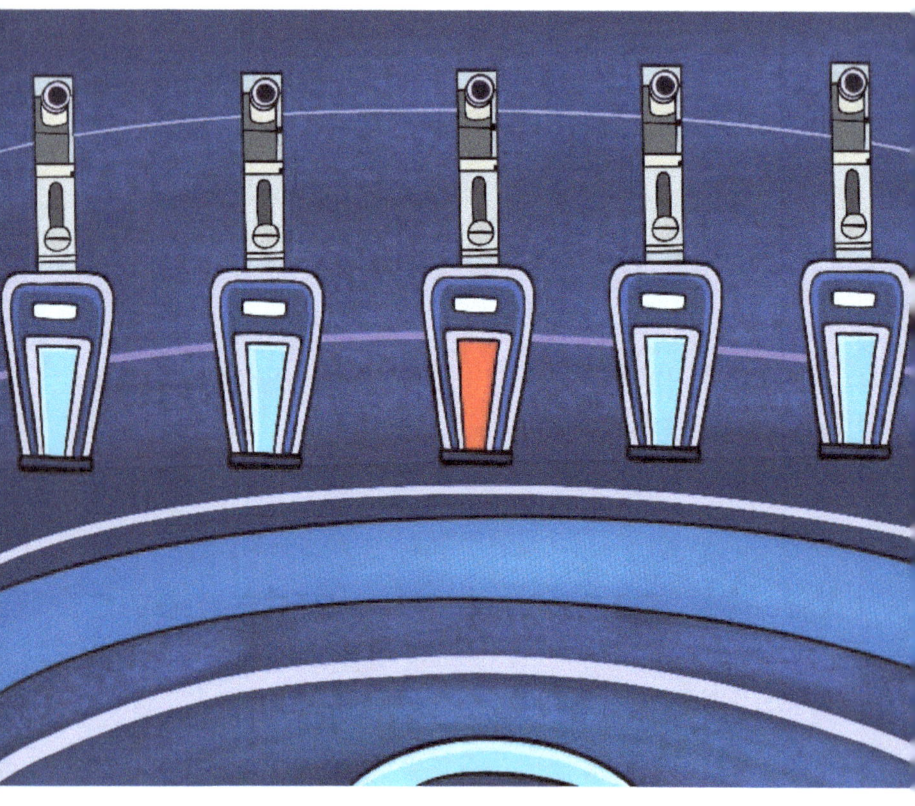

The Weakest Test Link.

What is a cable's favorite movie?

The Cable Guy.

CHAPTER 4

Why did the two commissioning engineers start a relationship?

It was love at first site.

Why are commissioning engineers comfortable with being double vaccinated?

Because they perform secondary injections daily.

What is a commissioning engineer's favorite movie genre?

The Wild Test.

What does a SCADA engineer eat for breakfast?

Serial.

Why do SCADA engineers love breakfast?

Lots of fibre.

What do you call a SCADA engineer wearing roller blades?

A rollerSCADA.

Why did the electrical engineer cross the road?

It was a short cir-cut.

WYE-WYE DO ALL GOOD THINGS END?

If these jokes hit close to Ohm, then please consider leaving a review on Amazon so others can discover this book!

WATTS NEXT?

Hopefully more crap electrical jokes…

Have your own electrical joke and want to share it?

Send them to matt@engineer-injokes.com

or visit www.engineer-injokes.com

If they're as lame as these, we'll post them in a future volume and credit you with the joke!

ABOUT THE AUTHOR

Matthew Pepe is an electrical engineer specializing in secondary and protection systems. Having spent more than a decade living in the world of substations, Matthew knows the ins and outs of the power industry – and all of the groanworthy jokes that come with it. If he's not working on power projects, he's brainstorming the next crap joke or lame pun to ruin his fellow colleague's day. This book combines his passion for engineering and humor, hoping that it brings a few laughs to everyone in the field.

www.ingramcontent.com/pod-product-compliance
Lightning Source LLC
Chambersburg PA
CBHW061745050726
47598CB00002B/592